Quinn,
be courageous enough to always
chase after what you want.

Quinn Starts School
Written by Erin Martens
Illustrated by Carol Karimi

Copyright © 2025 Erin Martens

All rights reserved. No part of this book may be reproduced in any manner whatsoever without prior written permission of the publisher.

First Printing, 2025

Published by Little Ones Wellness
www.littleoneswellness.com
Instagram @little_ones_wellness

ISBN Hardcover: 9781763776906
ISBN Paperback: 9781763776913
ISBN Hardcover V2: 9781763776920

At last, it was Quinn's first day of school.
A day she'd been dreaming would be really cool.

But now that the time was finally here,
fluttering feelings began to appear.

Quinn ate her breakfast and then brushed her hair.

On went the clothes
she'd been begging to wear.

Mum had her lunchbox all ready to go.
Dad gave a hug and straightened her bow.

Quivering lips, nerves started to show.

"Mummy and Daddy,
I don't want to go!"

Mum sang a song to help ease her fears,
while Dad blinked away his happy tears.

They reached the school gate
and waited a while.
Quinn tried to be brave
and worked hard to smile.

Hands were held tightly on the way to the door.
Nervous eyes glued to her new classroom floor.

"Hello, little Quinn. Miss Martens is my name. It's lovely to see you. Come, let's play a game".

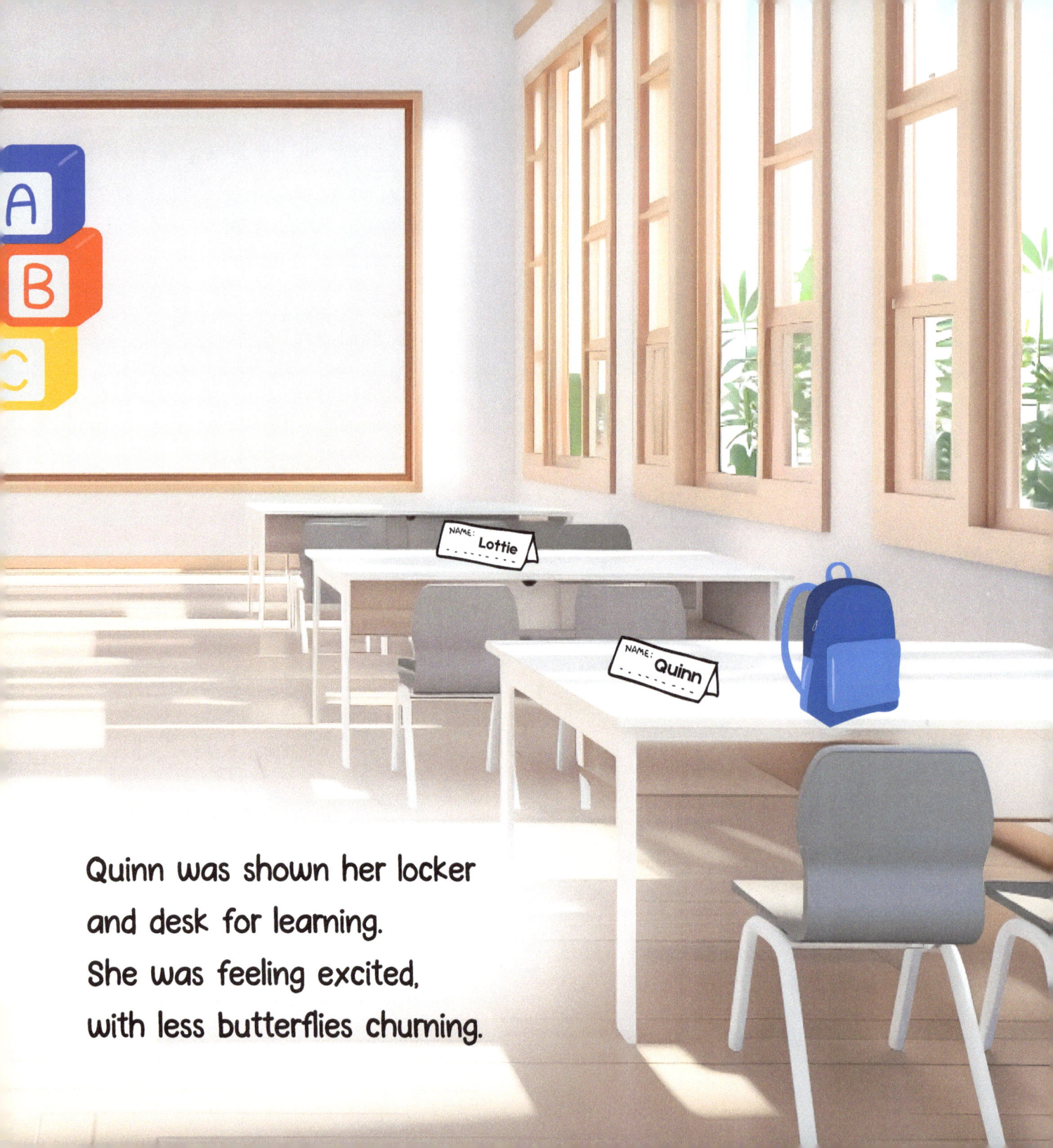

Quinn was shown her locker and desk for learning. She was feeling excited, with less butterflies churning.

Quinn shed a tear when Mum said goodbye. "You're being so brave", Dad wiped his eye.

She took a deep breath to help her nerves pass, so many new faces, 19 in the class.

Quinn had been worried about
making new friends,
she was afraid she'd be lonely
until the day ends.

A little voice said
"Hi, I'm Lottie and this is Finn"
and that sparked a new friendship
for Finn, Lottie and Quinn.

The bell rang loudly,
school had now begun.
"Come sit on the floor,
we're in for some fun".

ABCDEFGHIJKLMNOPQRSTUVWXYZ

Welcome to your first day

Then Miss Martens called out each name.
One by one, "**Here!**",
the kids would exclaim.

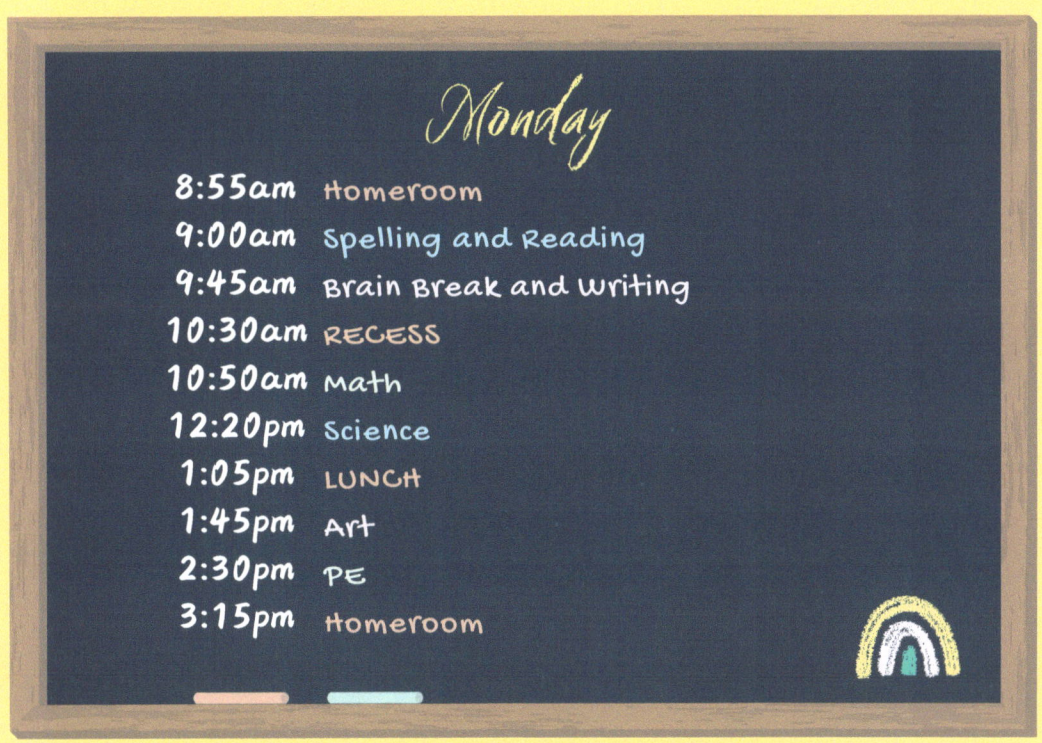

She then talked through the plans for the day,
Quinn listened carefully, her nerves fading away.

Miss Martens explained the rules for the class,
like raising your hand if you have a question to ask.

Spelling was the first lesson of the day, they explored some new sounds like 'oa' and 'ay'.

Next, a quick break to munch on some fruit.
Then **dancing** and **moving**, the kids had a hoot!

Feeling fresh, it was time for some writing.
Tracing their names, **oh** this was **exciting!**

Before they knew it, the recess bell rang, and little Quinn wanted a place to hang.

She worked up the courage and asked to join in,
and away she went playing with Lottie and Finn.

The bell rang, bringing recess to an end,
lining up at the door, next to a friend.

Back to the floor to listen intently.
Math was up next, there were numbers aplenty!

Learning to count beads... "Anything below twenty.
No more than that please, that's certainly plenty!".

All of a sudden, Quinn needed the toilet.
She couldn't hold on. She couldn't ignore it.

She raised up her hand while Miss Martens was talking.
A nod of her head and Quinn was out walking.

Returning to class as fast as she could.
Straight back to her work, like she knew she should.

Science was up next and Quinn was excited.
Unsure what to expect, should she be frightened?

"Today, we're learning about our five senses.
What are the five, are there any guesses?"

Sight, taste, sound, smell and touch.

Only one lesson in and they have all learnt so much!

When Science finished, it was time for some lunch.
Out came the lunchboxes...

munch, sip, crunch.

After eating, it's time to go outside
to make some new friends
or play on the slide.

Back to the classroom and straight into Art.
This was the class Quinn was excited to start.
Exploring with some paints, crayons or clay,
it's time to create a colourful display.

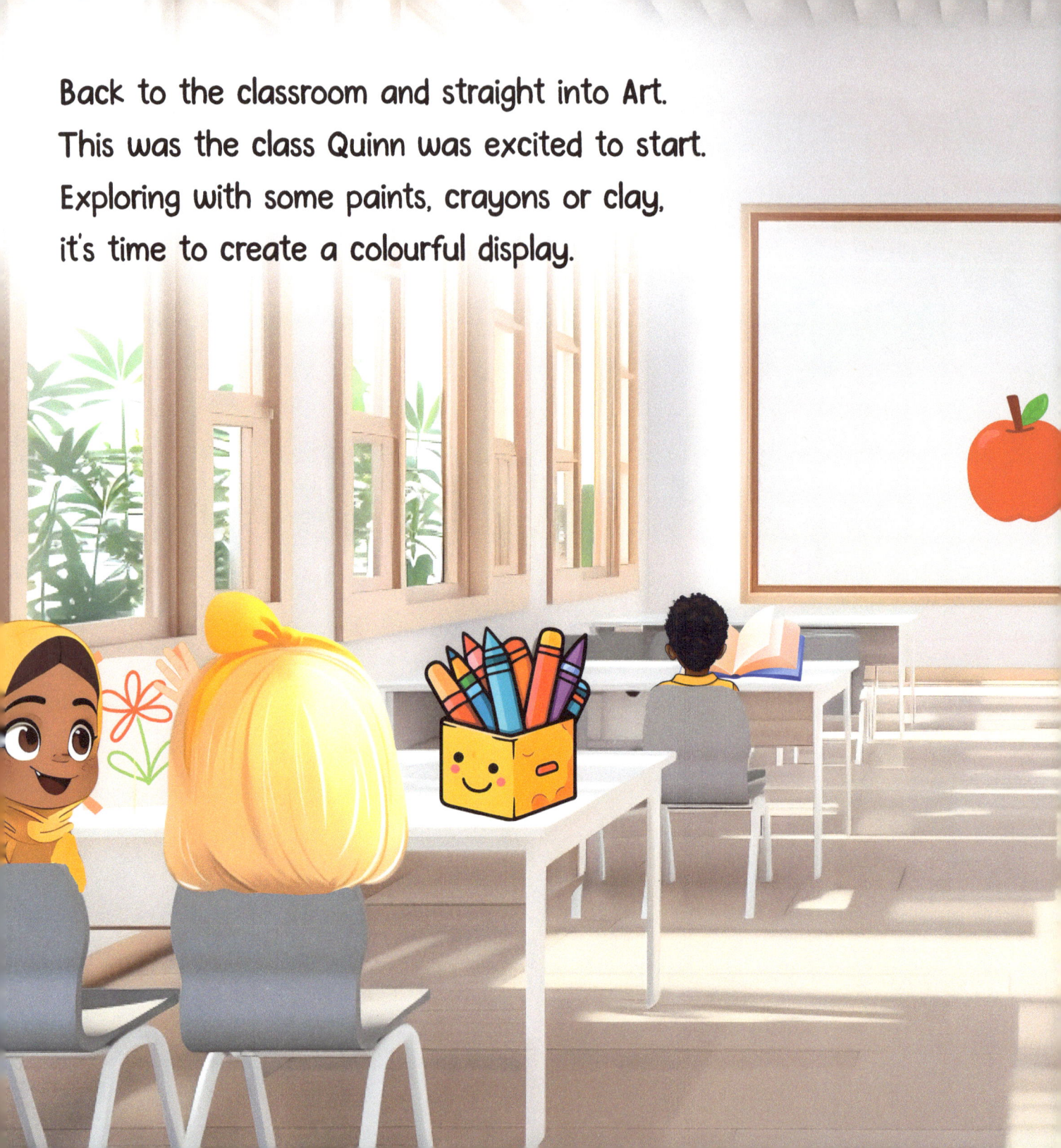

Before the day's end, the kids did PE, running and jumping, they all felt so free!

The final bell rang and Quinn skipped outside.
She spotted her parents, all filled with pride.

"I'm so proud of you". Dad said with a grin.
"Each day will get easier, I promise you, Quinn".

Write about your first day of school...

www.ingramcontent.com/pod-product-compliance
Lightning Source LLC
Chambersburg PA
CBHW041521070526
44585CB00002B/32